snacks

sweet and savoury treats

Yasa Boga

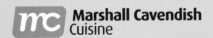
Marshall Cavendish
Cuisine

Translation by Ilona Pitt
Design by Steven Tan
Photography by Soerjanto Photography

Copyright © 2010 Marshall Cavendish International (Asia) Private Limited

Published by Marshall Cavendish Cuisine
An imprint of Marshall Cavendish International
1 New Industrial Road, Singapore 536196

Other Marshall Cavendish Offices:
Marshall Cavendish International. PO Box 65829, London, EC1P 1NY, UK • Marshall Cavendish Corporation, 99 White Plains Road, Tarrytown NY 10591-9001, USA • Marshall Cavendish International (Thailand) Co Ltd. 253 Asoke, 12th Flr, Sukhumvit 21 Road, Klongtoey Nua, Wattana, Bangkok 10110, Thailand • Marshall Cavendish (Malaysia) Sdn Bhd, Times Subang, Lot 46, Subang Hi-Tech Industrial Park, Batu Tiga, 40000 Shah Alam, Selangor Darul Ehsan, Malaysia

Marshall Cavendish is a trademark of Times Publishing Limited

National Library Board, Singapore Cataloguing-in-Publication Data

Yasa Boga (Group)
Snacks : sweet and savoury treats / Yasa Boga. – Singapore : Marshall Cavendish Cuisine, c2010.
p. cm. – (Home cooking)
ISBN-13 : 978-981-4302-25-8

1. Snack foods – Indonesia. 2. Cookery, Indonesian. I. Title.
II. Series: Home cooking.

TX724.5.I5
641.53909598 – dc22   OCN639722348

Printed in Malaysia by Times Offset (M) Sdn Bhd

contents

introduction

There is an endless variety of Indonesian-style snacks to satisfy your taste buds. Some varieties are sweet and rich while others are savoury with crispy or soft textures. In this cookbook, we have categorised the snacks according to the types of flour used.

Other than plain (all-purpose) flour, Asian snacks are also made with the use of rice flour, glutinous rice flour, mung bean flour, sago flour and other base ingredients such as cassava, sweet potato and corn.

For those new to Indonesian cooking, we have provided some tips on achieving delicious and visually appealing snacks. As you run through the recipes, you will also realise that most of the ingredients used are easily obtainable from the Asian section of any supermarket. The same applies for cooking utensils— simply improvise with whatever is available in your kitchen.

Indonesian snacks typically have a short shelf life. If properly stored in the fridge, most of these snacks can be kept for up to two days. Snacks which contain rice flour, glutinous rice flour and sago flour will regain their chewy textures when reheated by steaming.

ingredients

Flours

Rice flour, glutinous rice flour, mung bean flour, cassava flour, sago flour and plain (all-purpose) flour are generally used in snack recipes. All these types of flour are easily available, whether from a traditional wet market or the Asian products section of any supermarket.

After opening, it is best to store packages of flour in airtight containers in cool, shaded areas to retain their freshness. For better end results, it is also advisable to sift and sun-dry the flour in a bamboo basket prior to using.

Grated Coconut

Grated coconut is often used for coating snacks. Choose a half-ripe coconut and scrape off its thin, brown layer of skin, then grate the coconut sideways. Mix a little salt into the grated coconut and steam for about 10 minutes. This will prevent the grated coconut from spoiling easily in warm and humid weather.

Alternatively, grated coconut can be purchased from wet markets and supermarkets.

Coconut Cream and Milk

Coconut cream and milk are extracted from grated coconut. Coconut cream is more concentrated than coconut milk as less water is used in the extraction.

To obtain coconut cream, add 200 ml (7 fl oz / $^4/_5$ cup) warm water to one grated coconut, then knead and squeeze mixture and strain with a cheesecloth. To obtain coconut milk, use a larger amount of water.

Ready-packed coconut cream and milk are available in powder, cream and liquid form. Follow the directions for use given on the packaging.

Glutinous Rice

Two different varieties of glutinous rice are available—white and black. Glutinous rice should be soaked in water for about 2–3 hours before cooking. The glutinous rice grains will then cook through easily but still retain a chewy texture. While the usual rice grains can be half-cooked prior to their use in recipes where further steaming is required, glutinous rice has to be fully cooked before it is subjected to further processing in recipes as the grains may otherwise not cook through. To cook glutinous rice, steam the grains over high heat for about 20 minutes until the rice is translucent and cooked through.

Sweeteners

Palm sugar is used in many of these recipes for its rich and aromatic flavour. There are several variaties of palm sugar; yellow palm sugar is processed from coconut flower essence and a darker coloured sugar is processed from the *siwalan* or *aren* palm flower essence. Always use premium quality palm sugar as an inferior product may contain sago flour which may cause the texture of the snacks to be tough.

Food Colouring and Flavours

In general, many Indonesian snacks use a natural green food colouring which is obtained from the juice of *suji* leaves. If *suji* leaves are not readily available, substitute with a few drops of green *pandan* extract or artificial green food colouring.

Turmeric juice is a natural source of yellow food colouring while the blue pea (*teleng*) flower (Clitoria ternatea) is a source of natural blue food colouring. To obtain pink and other shades of colour, artificial food colourings are used.

The predominant flavours in these Indonesian snacks are derived from coconut milk or *pandan* leaves. In some recipes, ground vanilla, jackfruit, durian, kaffir lime leaves or lemongrass contribute a unique flavour to the snacks.

utensils

Steamer

A 30-cm (12-in) diameter round steamer is ideal as it can accommodate a 20-cm (8-in) square tin and is large enough to hold about 10 leaf-wrapped snacks or small bowls. Check also that the steamer comes with a metal disk with large perforations to allow strong steam to rise through for steaming the snacks quickly. A metal plate with tiny perforations is more suitable for steaming rice as you can spread the rice grains directly on the plate for steaming.

Always cover the top tier or line the rim of the steamer with a cotton tea towel before steaming to prevent excess moisture forming on the inside of the lid and dripping onto the food.

Special Moulds

Special moulds are needed when making some of these snacks, namely Indonesian Waffles, Mud Cakes, Colourful Rice Flour Cakes, Indonesian Muffins and Mung Bean Cakes. These special moulds can be found in Asian markets and baking stores, but if they are not available, Indonesian Waffles, Mud Cakes and Indonesian Muffins can be made using an electric waffle mould or electric Dutch pancake pan. The down side, of course, is that you cannot vary the shapes of the cakes.

Baking Tins/Glass Dishes

For snacks that are made in large tin or dishes, then cut to size, such as with Layered Cake, Sweet Glutinous Rice, Custard Rice Cakes and Baked Rice Flour Cake, we recommend using square aluminium tins and round or square glass dishes with a height of 4-cm (2-in) Do note that layered cakes such as Jackfruit Pudding and Sweet Potato Cakes can also be made in individual portions in small glass bowls or ramekins.

Leaves for Wrapping

Several types of Indonesian snacks are wrapped in leaves prior to cooking, with coconut leaves and banana leaves being the most common.

Before using, dip the leaves in boiling water for 1–2 seconds to make them malleable, so they are less likely to tear when folded. Alternatively, leave the leaves in the sun for about 15 minutes or scald them for 1–2 minutes over a flame before using.

Clorot　　Lapek Bugis　　Tum

cooking techniques

Kneading

This is done to introduce as much air into the mixture as possible, so the texture of the snack is smooth and soft. Kneading will also enable the mixture to expand well if the recipe requires fermentation.

Kneading is done by hand, by repeatedly pressing and pushing the mixture forward with your palms until the mixture is soft and malleable, with a smooth and matte texture, and no longer sticks to your hands.

Steaming

Before steaming snacks that are not wrapped in leaves, wrap the inside of the steamer lid with a cotton tea towel and make sure that the water in the steamer is sufficient and rapidly boiling. Otherwise, hot water droplets will fall from the inside of the lid onto the surface of the snacks and result in them hardening. Furthermore, the snacks may be prevented from expanding to their optimal sizes by the water droplets.

weights and measures

Quantities for this book are given in Metric, Imperial and American (spoon) measures. Standard spoon and cup measurements used are: 1 tsp = 5 ml, 1 Tbsp = 15 ml, 1 cup = 250 ml. All measures are level unless otherwise stated.

LIQUID AND VOLUME MEASURES

Metric	Imperial	American
5 ml	1/6 fl oz	1 teaspoon
10 ml	1/3 fl oz	1 dessertspoon
15 ml	1/2 fl oz	1 tablespoon
60 ml	2 fl oz	1/4 cup (4 tablespoons)
85 ml	2 1/2 fl oz	1/4 cup
90 ml	3 fl oz	3/8 cup (6 tablespoons)
125 ml	4 fl oz	1/2 cup
180 ml	6 fl oz	3/4 cup
250 ml	8 fl oz	1 cup
300 ml	10 fl oz (1/2 pint)	1 1/4 cups
375 ml	12 fl oz	1 1/2 cups
435 ml	14 fl oz	1 3/4 cups
500 ml	16 fl oz	2 cups
625 ml	20 fl oz (1 pint)	2 1/2 cups
750 ml	24 fl oz (1 1/5 pints)	3 cups
1 litre	32 fl oz (1 3/5 pints)	4 cups
1.25 litres	40 fl oz (2 pints)	5 cups
1.5 litres	48 fl oz (2 2/5 pints)	6 cups
2.5 litres	80 fl oz (4 pints)	10 cups

DRY MEASURES

Metric	Imperial
30 grams	1 ounce
45 grams	1 1/2 ounces
55 grams	2 ounces
70 grams	2 1/2 ounces
85 grams	3 ounces
100 grams	3 1/2 ounces
110 grams	4 ounces
125 grams	4 1/2 ounces
140 grams	5 ounces
280 grams	10 ounces
450 grams	16 ounces (1 pound)
500 grams	1 pound, 1 1/2 ounces
700 grams	1 1/2 pounds
800 grams	1 3/4 pounds
1 kilogram	2 pounds, 3 ounces
1.5 kilograms	3 pounds, 4 1/2 ounces
2 kilograms	4 pounds, 6 ounces

OVEN TEMPERATURE

	°C	°F	Gas Regulo
Very slow	120	250	1
Slow	150	300	2
Moderately slow	160	325	3
Moderate	180	350	4
Moderately hot	190/200	370/400	5/6
Hot	210/220	410/440	6/7
Very hot	230	450	8
Super hot	250/290	475/550	9/10

LENGTH

Metric	Imperial
0.5 cm	1/4 inch
1 cm	1/2 inch
1.5 cm	3/4 inch
2.5 cm	1 inch

jackfruitpudding

Green Layer

Cooking oil for greasing tin

150 g (5$^1/_3$ oz) rice flour

50 g (1$^2/_3$ oz) sugar

300 ml (10 fl oz / 1$^1/_4$ cups) coconut milk, extracted from $^1/_2$ grated coconut

$^1/_2$ tsp salt

5 *pandan* + 10 *suji* leaves blended with 50 ml (1$^2/_3$ fl oz / $^1/_4$ cup) water, liquid strained

Plain Coconut Milk Layer

300 ml (10 fl oz / 1$^1/_4$ cups) coconut milk, extracted from $^1/_2$ grated coconut

20 g ($^2/_3$ oz) rice flour

$^1/_2$ tsp salt

150 g (5$^1/_3$ oz) ripe jackfruit, diced

- Prepare a 20-cm (8-in) square tin. Grease with cooking oil and place in a steamer. Set steamer over medium heat and bring water in steamer to the boil.

- Prepare green layer. Add all ingredients to a mixing bowl and stir evenly until combined. Pour mixture into tin and steam for about 20 minutes until cooked.

- While waiting for green layer to cook, prepare plain coconut milk layer. Mix all ingredients together in a medium pot except jackfruit. Stir and cook over low heat until mixture has thickened. Remove from heat.

- Pour mixture on top of green layer and sprinkle jackfruit over. Steam again for about 45 minutes until cake is fully cooked. Remove and leave to cool. Cut and serve as desired.

NOTE:

If preferred, jackfruit pudding can be made in individual portions with the use of small glass bowls or ramekins. Simply follow the above steps in making the two mixtures and divide them equally among the bowls or ramekins.

bananacakes

2 large (horn) bananas, peeled and
steamed whole for about 5 minutes

125 g (4^1/$_2$ oz) mung bean flour

1.25 litres (40 fl oz / 5 cups) coconut milk,
extracted from 1^1/$_2$ grated coconuts

200 g (7 oz) sugar

1 tsp vanilla extract or ^{1}/$_4$ tsp ground vanilla

^{1}/$_4$ tsp salt

25 banana leaves or clear plastic sheets
for wrapping, each 15 x 15-cm (6 x 6-in)

- Slice steamed bananas into 1-cm (^{1}/$_2$-in) thick rounds. Set aside.

- In a mixing bowl, combine mung bean flour with 500 ml (16 fl oz / 2 cups) coconut milk until flour has dissolved. Set aside.

- In a medium pot, combine remaining coconut milk, sugar, vanilla and salt. Stirring continuously, cook mixture over medium heat and bring to the boil. Add coconut milk-flour mixture and stir until mixture has thickened. Cake mixture is cooked when mixture starts to splutter.

- Assemble banana cakes. Place a slice of banana onto the centre of a banana leaf or plastic sheet. Top with 2 Tbsp cake mixture. Fold banana leaf or plastic sheet into a square parcel and tuck ends underneath neatly. Repeat until all ingredients are used up. Leave to set completely. Serve chilled or at room temperature.

layeredcake

500 g (1 lb 1^{1}/$_{2}$ oz) rice flour

300 g (11 oz) sugar

^{1}/$_{2}$ tsp salt

1 tsp *pandan* essence

1.1 litres (35^{1}/$_{2}$ fl oz / 4^{2}/$_{5}$ cups) coconut milk, extracted from 1 grated coconut

1–2 drops each food colouring in 3 different colours

Cooking oil for greasing tin

- In a large mixing bowl, combine flour, sugar, salt and *pandan* essence. Gradually add coconut milk and knead until mixture becomes smooth. When the last portion of coconut milk has been added to mixture and a thick batter forms, stir evenly with a wooden spoon until smooth.

- Divide batter into 3 equal portions. Stir in food colouring for each portion as desired.

- Grease a 15-cm (6-in) square tin with oil and place in a preheated steamer. Ladle 50 ml (1^{2}/$_{3}$ fl oz / ^{1}/$_{4}$ cup) of coloured batter into tin, and steam for about 5 minutes until set.

- Repeat step with remaining 2 portions of batters, alternating among different coloured batters until all portions are used up. Steam whole cake for up to 1 hour until cake is fully cooked. Remove and leave to cool. Cut into desired shapes and serve.

NOTE:

Do not forget to wrap the steamer lid with a cotton tea towel to prevent hot water droplets from dripping onto the cake surface which will cause the cake to harden.

colourfulriceflourcakes

250 g (9 oz) rice flour

125 g (4¹/₂ oz) sugar

¹/₂ tsp salt

375 ml (12 fl oz / 1¹/₂ cups) warm coconut
milk, extracted from ¹/₂ grated coconut

¹/₂ egg, whisked

1–2 drops each red, green and brown
food colouring

- In a large mixing bowl, combine rice flour, sugar and salt. Add 4 Tbsp warm coconut milk to mixture and knead for about 15 minutes until mixture is no longer sticky.

- Gradually add remaining coconut milk and continue to knead mixture. When the last portion of coconut milk has been added to mixture and a thick batter forms, stir evenly with a wooden spoon until smooth. Add whisked egg and stir to combine well. Cover bowl with a tea towel and set aside for about 30 minutes.

- Halve batter portions. Set one-half portion aside. Further divide one-half portion of batter into 3 equal parts, then add food colouring to each part accordingly.

- Heat *carabikang* moulds until hot and smoking. Fill each mould with plain batter until two-thirds full and top each mould with a little coloured batter to form different coloured cakes. Cook until tiny holes appear on surface of cakes and sides of cakes are dry.

- Loosen cakes with a bamboo skewer and remove to a plate. Gently pull each cake around the edges until they open up like 'flowers'.

- Repeat until all ingredients are used up.

cornpudding

40 broad *pandan* leaves for making square casings

Stapler and staples

Top Layer

2 Tbsp rice flour

2 Tbsp corn flour (cornstarch)

1 tsp salt

500 ml (16 fl oz / 2 cups) coconut cream, extracted from 1$\frac{1}{2}$ grated coconuts

Bottom Layer

150 g (5$\frac{1}{3}$ oz) rice flour

100 g (3$\frac{1}{2}$ oz) corn flour (cornstarch)

500 ml (16 fl oz / 2 cups) water + 7 knotted *pandan* leaves, boiled for 20 minutes

250 g (9 oz) sugar

300 g (11 oz) canned corn kernels, drained

- Prepare *pandan* leaf casings. Snip along each length of *pandan* leaf halfway, from edge to central vein at 4-cm (1$\frac{3}{4}$-in) intervals. Make 4 cuts in total. Fold along the 4 cuts to form a box-like casing and staple to secure. Set aside.

- Prepare bottom layer. In a mixing bowl, combine rice and corn flours with 250 ml (8 fl oz / 1 cup) *pandan* leaf water until flours have dissolved. In a medium pot, add remaining *pandan* leaf water, dissolved flour mixture, sugar and corn kernels. Cook over low heat, stirring continuously until mixture thickens. Set aside.

- Prepare top layer. Combine all ingredients in a medium pot and cook over low heat, stirring continuously until mixture thickens. Remove from heat.

- Assemble corn pudding. Fill each *pandan* leaf casing with corn mixture until two-thirds full. Spoon top-layer mixture over to fill up casings and level surfaces gently with the back of a metal spoon. Decorate as desired and serve.

youngcoconutdessert

2 *pandan* leaves, cut diagonally into 3-cm (1½-in) strips

125 g (4½ oz) palm sugar, finely grated

500 ml (16 fl oz / 2 cups) coconut cream, extracted from 1 grated coconut

250 g (9 oz) young coconut flesh, shredded

20 banana leaves for making parcels (*tum*), each 20 x 30-cm (8 x 12-in)

Bamboo skewers

Green Cake Mixture

250 g (9 oz) rice flour

2 Tbsp sago flour

100 g (3½ oz) sugar

½ tsp salt

800 ml (26 fl oz / 3¼ cups) coconut milk, extracted from 1 grated coconut

10 *suji* leaves blended with 100 ml (3½ fl oz / ⅖ cup) water, liquid strained

- Prepare green cake mixture. In a mixing bowl, combine rice and sago flours, sugar, salt, 300 ml (10 fl oz / 1¼ cups) coconut milk and *suji* leaf water until flours have dissolved. Set aside. In a medium pot, cook remaining coconut milk over medium heat, stirring constantly and bring to the boil. Reduce heat and add flour mixture. Stirring constantly, cook until mixture thickens. Remove from heat and set aside.

- Assemble parcels. Stack 2 banana leaves together, with shiny sides facing outwards. Place a strip of *pandan* leaf in centre of leaves. Top with 1 Tbsp palm sugar and 2 Tbsp green cake mixture.

- Wrap and fold leaves into a *tum* (page 11). Spoon 2 Tbsp coconut cream followed by 1–2 Tbsp coconut flesh into parcel and secure with a bamboo skewer. Repeat until all ingredients are used up. Steam for about 30 minutes until cooked.

NOTE:

If fresh suji leaves are not available, add 2–3 drops green food colouring to 100 ml (3½ fl oz / ⅖ cup) water and stir to mix well.

rice flour bread

250 g (9 oz) rice flour

50 g (1²/₃ oz) sago flour

6 g (¹/₈ oz) instant yeast

125 g (4¹/₂ oz) sugar

¹/₄ tsp salt

250 ml (8 fl oz / 1 cup) coconut milk, obtained from second squeezing

250 ml (8 fl oz / 1 cup) coconut cream, extracted from 1 grated coconut

Cooking oil for greasing tin

Coconut Sauce

500 ml (16 fl oz / 2 cups) coconut milk, extracted from ¹/₂ grated coconut

100 g (3¹/₂ oz) palm sugar, finely grated

25 g (³/₄ oz) sugar

2 *pandan* leaves

¹/₄ tsp salt

1 Tbsp corn flour (cornstarch) + 2 tsp water

- Prepare coconut sauce. Except corn flour mixture, combine all ingredients in a medium pot. Cook over medium heat while stirring constantly and bring to the boil. Remove and strain mixture. Return strained mixture to pot and bring to the boil, then thicken with corn flour mixture. Remove from heat and leave to cool.

- In a mixing bowl, combine all ingredients except coconut milk and cream. Gradually add coconut milk and knead mixture for about 30 minutes until sugar has dissolved. Cover bowl with a tea towel and leave for 1 hour in a warm place until mixture has doubled in volume.

- Gradually add coconut cream to leavened mixture, stirring constantly with a wooden spoon to form a thick batter.

- Grease a 20 x 7-cm (8 x 3-in) square tin with oil and preheat it in a steamer for about 5 minutes.

- Pour batter into preheated tin and steam for about 30 minutes until cooked. Remove and leave to cool. Slice as desired and serve with coconut sauce.

lumpang cake

Cooking oil for greasing bowls

100 g (3^1/$_2$ oz) rice flour

30 g (1 oz) sago flour

50 g (1^2/$_3$ oz) sugar

150 ml (5 fl oz / ^{3}/$_5$ cup) water

10 *suji* leaves blended with 50 ml (1^2/$_3$ fl oz /
^{1}/$_4$ cup) water, liquid strained

^{1}/$_2$ tsp salt

^{1}/$_2$ skinned young coconut, grated and mixed
with ^{1}/$_4$ tsp salt, then steamed for 10 minutes

- Grease 20 small heatproof (flameproof) bowls or porcelain moulds with cooking oil. Arrange bowls or moulds in steamer. Cover and preheat steamer for 15–20 minutes over medium heat until water in steamer boils rapidly.

- Except for grated coconut, combine all ingredients in a mixing bowl and stir until mixture is smooth. Strain mixture with a metal strainer.

- Ladle strained mixture into preheated bowls or moulds until they are three-quarters full. Stir well before ladling mixture into each bowl to prevent mixture from clumping. Steam for 45 minutes until cooked. Unmould and serve with grated coconut.

NOTE:

If fresh suji leaves are not available, add 1–2 drops green food colouring to 50 ml (1^2/$_3$ fl oz / ^{1}/$_4$ cup) water and stir to mix well.

bowl-shaped cakes

$1/2$ tsp instant yeast + 50 g ($1^2/_3$ oz) rice flour +
50 ml ($1^3/_4$ oz) warm water, combined by hand and
set aside for 15 minutes

250 g (9 oz) rice flour

75 g ($2^2/_3$ oz) sago flour

$1/4$ tsp salt

200 ml ($6^1/_2$ fl oz / $4/_5$ cup) coconut milk, extracted
from $1/2$ grated coconut

1–2 drops food colouring of choice

Coconut Syrup

350 g (12 oz) sugar

400 ml ($13^1/_2$ fl oz / $1^2/_3$ cups) young coconut water

- Prepare coconut syrup. Heat coconut water in a pan and add sugar, stirring until sugar is dissolved. Leave to cool.

- In a mixing bowl, combine yeast mixture, rice and sago flours and salt. Gradually add coconut milk while kneading constantly. While kneading, gradually add coconut syrup and continue to knead mixture for 30 minutes until smooth. Cover bowl with a tea towel and set aside for 3 hours.

- Divide leavened mixture into 2–3 equal portions and add food colouring to each portion as desired.

- Grease 20 small heatproof (flameproof) moulds with cooking oil. Arrange moulds in steamer. Cover and preheat steamer for 15–20 minutes over medium heat until water in steamer boils rapidly. Ensure there is sufficient boiling water in steamer before steaming cakes.

- Fill preheated moulds with mixture until they are three-quarters full. Steam for about 30 minutes without lifting steamer lid. Remove and unmould cakes. Leave to cool and serve as desired.

NOTE:

To make brown-coloured bowl-shaped cakes, replace regular sugar in coconut syrup with palm sugar.

string**hoppers**

250 g (8 oz) rice flour

$^1/_2$ tsp salt

550 ml (18$^2/_3$ fl oz / 2$^1/_4$ cups) boiling water

1–2 drops food colouring of choice

Banana leaves for lining steamer

Coconut Sauce

500 ml (16 fl oz / 2 cups) coconut milk, extracted from 1 grated coconut

150 g (5$^1/_3$ oz) palm sugar, finely grated

$^1/_4$ tsp salt

2 *pandan* leaves, knotted

$^1/_2$ tsp corn flour (cornstarch) + 1 Tbsp water

- Line perforated disk of steamer with a piece of muslin cloth and steam rice flour for about 1 hour. Transfer steamed flour to a mixing bowl and add salt and boiling water. Stir evenly with a wooden spoon until combined. When mixture is cool enough, knead by hand until smooth.

- Divide mixture into 3 equal portions. Leave 1 portion plain, and add food colouring to each of the remaining 2 portions as desired. Put mixtures through a *putu mayang* press to obtain thin, noodle-like strands of dough. Line steamer strainer with banana leaves and grease with cooking oil. Arrange dough strands on top and steam for about 20 minutes until cooked.

- Prepare coconut sauce. Except corn flour mixture, combine all ingredients in a medium pot. Stirring constantly, cook over medium heat and bring to the boil. Thicken sauce with corn flour mixture and return to the boil again.

- Remove from heat and discard *pandan* leaves. Serve string hoppers with coconut sauce as desired.

riceflourcones

Coconut leaves for wrapping, spines removed

Bamboo skewers to secure

100 ml ($3^1/_3$ fl oz / $^2/_5$ cup) water

150 g ($5^1/_3$ oz) palm sugar, finely grated

$^1/_4$ tsp salt

250 ml (8 fl oz / 1 cup) coconut milk, extracted from $^1/_2$ grated coconut

50 g ($1^2/_3$ oz) rice flour + 50 g ($1^2/_3$ oz) sago flour, sifted

- Prepare *clorot* cone wrappers (page 11). Secure each cone with a skewer at the mouth. Make sure the tip of each cone is pointed and tight to prevent leaf from unravelling. Set aside.

- In a small pot, heat water, palm sugar and salt until sugar has dissolved. Remove from heat and strain sugar syrup. Combine sugar syrup with coconut milk and stir to mix well.

- Transfer sifted flours to a mixing bowl. Gradually add coconut milk mixture to flour mixture, stirring constantly, until mixture is smooth and combined.

- Preheat steamer equipped with a steaming disk with large perforations. When ready, stick cones in an upright position into holes of steaming disk, leaving gaps in between. Spoon mixture into cones until three-quarters full. Steam for 15 minutes until cakes are cooked.

- Alternatively, scatter used coconut pulp on a steaming disk lined with banana leaves. Stick cones in an upright position into bed of coconut pulp, leaving gaps in between. Spoon mixture into cones and steam as required.

crowncakes

Cakes

$\frac{1}{2}$ tsp instant yeast + 50 g (1$\frac{2}{3}$ oz) rice flour + 50 ml (1$\frac{2}{3}$ fl oz / $\frac{1}{4}$ cup) warm water, evenly mixed by hand and left aside for 15 minutes

250 g (9 oz) rice flour

75 g (2$\frac{2}{3}$ oz) sago flour

200 ml (6$\frac{1}{2}$ fl oz / $\frac{3}{4}$ cup) coconut milk, extracted from $\frac{1}{2}$ grated coconut

$\frac{1}{4}$ tsp salt

1–2 drops each red and green food colouring

Cooking oil for greasing bowls

Coconut Syrup

350 g (12 oz) sugar

400 ml (13$\frac{1}{2}$ fl oz / 1$\frac{2}{3}$ cup) young coconut water

Coconut Cream Mixture

50 g (1$\frac{2}{3}$ oz) rice flour

$\frac{1}{2}$ tsp salt

$\frac{1}{2}$ Tbsp sugar (optional)

300 ml (10 fl oz / 1$\frac{1}{4}$ cup) coconut cream, extracted from 1$\frac{1}{2}$ grated coconuts

- Prepare coconut syrup. Heat sugar and coconut juice together until sugar has dissolved totally. Set aside.

- Prepare coconut cream mixture. In a mixing bowl, combine all ingredients and stir until mixture is smooth. Set aside.

- Prepare cakes. In a separate mixing bowl, combine yeast mixture with rice and sago flours, coconut milk and salt, then knead by hand. While kneading, gradually add coconut syrup and knead mixture for 30 minutes until smooth. Cover bowl with a tea towel and set aside for 3 hours. Divide leavened mixture into 2 equal parts and colour one part with red colouring and the other part with green colouring.

- Grease cake moulds with oil. Arrange in steamer and preheat for about 20 minutes. When ready, fill each mould with cake mixture until three-quarters full. Ensure there is sufficient rapidly boiling water in steamer before steaming cakes. Steam for about 30 minutes over medium heat without lifting steamer lid. Remove, unmould and leave to cool.

- Fill a separate set of greased, larger heat-proof (flameproof) bowls with coconut cream mixture until one-third full. Place a steamed cake into each bowl. Place bowls in preheated steamer and steam for 15–20 minutes until set. Remove, unmould and serve as desired

chickenriceflourcakes

800 ml (26 fl oz / 3 1/4 cups) coconut milk, extracted from 1 1/2 grated coconuts

250 g (9 oz) rice flour

2 Tbsp sago flour

100 g (3 1/2 oz) sugar

1/2 tsp salt

25 young banana leaves, each 25 x 7-cm (10 x 3-in)

Spice Paste

5 shallots, peeled

2 cloves garlic, peeled

1 tsp coriander seeds, toasted

1/2 tsp cumin seeds, toasted

1/2 tsp ground white pepper

2 Tbsp cooking oil

Filling

250 g (9 oz) cooked chicken breast, skinned and shredded

2 Tbsp instant coconut cream

2–3 Tbsp water

1/4 tsp salt, or to taste

1 tsp sugar, or to taste

- Prepare spice paste. Combine all ingredients except cooking oil in a blender until fine. In a medium frying pan, heat oil and fry spice paste until fragrant.

- Prepare filling. Add all ingredients to spice paste in frying pan and stir-fry over medium heat until liquid has reduced completely. Remove and set aside.

- Combine 400 ml (13 1/3 fl oz / 1 3/4 cups) coconut milk with rice and sago flours and stir until dissolved. In a medium pot, bring remaining coconut milk, sugar, salt and combined flour mixture to the boil. Stir until mixture has thickened. Remove from heat.

- Assemble rice cakes. Stack 2 strips of banana leaves together with shiny sides facing outwards. Fold one end of leaves upwards to form a cone. Spoon 1–2 Tbsp rice flour mixture into cone, followed by 1 tsp chicken filling, then cover filling with 1 Tbsp rice flour mixture. Fold excess leaves over to cover ingredients. Flatten cone to form a triangle, then fold leaves over to close triangular parcel. Continue to fold leaves following the triangular shape of the parcel. Sit parcels on open ends.

- Arrange parcels on a steaming plate with end of leaves on the bottom so that parcel will not unravel. Steam parcels over rapidly boiling water for about 20 minutes until cooked through.

- Remove from heat and serve.

ricecakeswithdriedprawns

2 large red chillies

1 clove garlic, peeled

$1/4$ tsp salt

Sugar to taste

2 Tbsp cooking oil

75 g ($2^2/_3$ oz) dried prawns (shrimps), soaked in hot water, drained and pounded

$1/2$ spring onion (scallion), thinly sliced

1 large red chilli, seeded and finely sliced for decoration

Chinese coriander (cilantro) leaves for decoration

Rice Cake Layer

100 g ($3^1/_2$ oz) rice flour

50 g ($1^2/_3$ oz) sago flour

1 Tbsp sugar

1 tsp salt

$1/2$ tsp ground white pepper

600 ml (20 fl oz / $2^1/_2$ cups) warm coconut milk, extracted from 1 grated coconut mixed with sufficient warm water

Rich Coconut Milk Layer

250 ml (8 fl oz / 1 cup) coconut milk, extracted from 1 grated coconut

4 Tbsp rice flour

$1/2$ tsp salt

- Grease 18 small square heatproof (flameproof) moulds with oil. Set aside.

- Grind chillies, garlic, salt and sugar to a paste. Heat oil and fry chilli paste until fragrant, then add dried prawns and spring onion. Stir-fry over low heat until mixture is dry. Set aside.

- Prepare rice cake layer. In a mixing bowl, combine rice and sago flours, sugar, salt and pepper. Gradually pour in 300 ml (10 fl oz / $1^1/_4$ cups) warm coconut milk and stir until combined. Bring remaining coconut milk to the boil. Remove from heat and pour into flour mixture, stirring constantly until a thick batter forms. Fill square moulds with mixture until two-thirds full. Steam in a preheated steamer over medium heat for about 20 minutes until cakes have set.

- Prepare rich coconut milk layer. In a mixing bowl, combine all ingredients together. Ladle mixture on top of steamed cakes to fill up moulds. Return cakes to the steamer and steam again for 5–10 minutes until cakes are cooked. Sprinkle on chilli-dried prawn mixture while cakes are still hot. Garnish with sliced chilli and coriander leaves as desired.

spicy**coconut**rice cakes

500 g (1 lb 1¹/₂ oz) glutinous rice, soaked in water for 2 hours

250 ml (8 fl oz / 1 cup) coconut milk, extracted from ¹/₄ grated coconut

1 tsp salt

2 *pandan* leaves, knotted

Spiced Grated Coconut

¹/₂ semi-old coconut, skinned and grated

25 g (³/₄ oz) dried prawns (shrimps), dry-toasted and finely ground

2 large red chillies, ground

2 cloves garlic, peeled and ground

2 kaffir lime leaves

1 tsp salt

1 Tbsp sugar

- Drain and rinse glutinous rice, then steam for 15 minutes. In a small pot, combine coconut milk, salt and *pandan* leaves. Heat and bring to the boil. Remove and discard *pandan* leaves.

- Gradually add coconut milk to steamed glutinous rice and stir evenly until coconut milk is fully absorbed into mixture. Return glutinous rice to steamer and steam again for 20–30 minutes until cooked. When cool enough to handle, divide rice into 20 portions and shape into balls with lightly greased hands, then flatten slightly. Place on a large sheet of greased banana leaf.

- Prepare spiced grated coconut. Except salt and sugar, stir-fry all ingredients in a nonstick frying pan without oil until mixture is dry and brown in colour. While still hot, grind coconut mixture, salt and sugar together until fine.

- Transfer ground coconut mixture to a large flat plate and coat rice cakes with spiced coconut mixture. Garnish and serve as desired.

triangularcakeswith palmsugar

2 Tbsp slaked lime + 100 ml ($3^1/3$ fl oz / $^2/_5$ cup) water, stirred until dissolved and left to stand until water is no longer cloudy before use

1 kg (2 lb 3 oz) white glutinous rice, washed and drained

60 strips banana leaves for wrapping, each 25 x 7-cm (10 x 3-in)

Kitchen string for securing

$^1/_2$ young coconut, skinned and grated + $^1/_4$ tsp salt, steamed for about 10 minutes

Palm Sugar Syrup

300 g (11 oz) palm sugar, grated

3 Tbsp sugar

125 ml (4 fl oz / $^1/_2$ cup) water

- Sprinkle 1 Tbsp slaked lime water all over glutinous rice and stir to mix well. Take a strip of banana leaf and fold ends upwards to form a cone. Fill with glutinous rice and fold excess leaf over to cover rice, then continue to fold along triangular parcel until you reach the end of the leaf. Take a second strip of leaf and wrap triangular parcel before securing with kitchen string. Repeat until rice is used up.

- Place banana leaf parcels in a large pot and add sufficient water to cover. Cook over medium heat and bring to the boil, then simmer rapidly for 2–3 hours; top with hot water to cover parcels if required. When cooked, drain and leave to cool.

- Prepare palm sugar syrup. In a small pot, combine all ingredients, then heat and bring to the boil. Reduce heat and simmer until mixture turns into a thick syrup. Remove and strain.

- To serve, unwrap rice cakes and coat with grated coconut. Drizzle with palm sugar syrup.

NOTE:

This snack can be made in triangular or cylindrical parcels. If making cylindrical parcels, secure both ends with bamboo skewers. When cooked, unwrap and slice into rounds before serving. When wrapping the glutinous rice parcels, the shiny side of the banana leaf should be facing inwards, that is, in contact with the glutinous rice; the surfaces of the rice cakes will then be tinged with an attractive pale green colour.

sweetglutinousrice

500 g (1 lb 1¹/₂ oz) white glutinous rice, soaked for 2 hours and drained

500 ml (16 fl oz / 2 cups) coconut milk, extracted from 1 grated coconut

200 g (7 oz) palm sugar, grated

2 Tbsp sugar

3 *pandan* leaves, knotted

¹/₂ tsp salt

- Steam glutinous rice for about 30 minutes until cooked. Remove and set aside.

- In a medium pot, combine all remaining ingredients together. Stirring constantly, cook over medium heat until mixture bubbles and thickens. Remove from heat, discard pandan leaves and strain mixture.

- Return strained mixture to pot and bring to a simmer over low heat. Add steamed glutinous rice and stir constantly until liquid is fully absorbed by rice. Make sure rice grains are well coated and glossy looking but not burnt.

- Line a 20-cm (8-in) square tin with banana leaf or cling film. Transfer glutinous rice mixture to tin and press down with the back of a spoon or fork to level surface. Leave to cool.

- When cool, cut into diamond shapes, then garnish and serve as desired. Alternatively, mould rice mixture by hand into oval shapes while rice is still warm.

stuffed jackfruit

250 g (9 oz) white glutinous rice, soaked for 2 hours and drained

125 ml (4 fl oz / ½ cup) coconut milk, extracted from ½ grated coconut

½ tsp salt

30 ripe jackfruit bulbs, slit on 1 side and stoned

Cooking oil for deep-frying

Palm Sugar Syrup

200 g (7 oz) palm sugar, grated

100 ml (3⅓ fl oz / ⅖ cup) water

Batter

150 g (5⅓ oz) plain (all-purpose) flour

1 egg, whisked

2 tsp sugar

250 ml (8 fl oz / 1 cup) water

- Drain and rinse glutinous rice, then steam for 15 minutes. In a small pot, combine coconut milk and salt. Heat and bring to the boil.

- Gradually add coconut milk to steamed glutinous rice and stir evenly until coconut milk is fully absorbed into mixture. Return glutinous rice to steamer and steam again for 20–30 minutes until cooked. When cool enough to handle, divide rice into 30 portions and place on a sheet of greased banana leaf.

- Stuff each jackfruit bulb with cooked glutinous rice. Set aside.

- Prepare palm sugar syrup. In a small pot, dissolve palm sugar with water, adjust according to taste, then heat and bring to the boil. Remove and strain. Return mixture to pot and simmer over low heat until mixture thickens. Set aside to cool.

- Prepare batter. In a mixing bowl, combine all ingredients and stir well to obtain a smooth mixture.

- Heat oil for deep-frying. Coat stuffed jackfruit bulbs with batter and lower into hot oil. Deep-fry battered jackfruit bulbs until golden brown in colour. Drain on paper towels and drizzle with palm sugar syrup before serving.

sweet**glutinous**rice balls

300 g (11 oz) glutinous rice flour

5 *pandan* + 10 *suji* leaves blended with
5 Tbsp water, liquid strained

A pinch of slaked lime + 2 tsp water, stir until
dissolved

100 g (3$^{1}/_{2}$ oz) palm sugar, finely grated

$^{1}/_{3}$ young coconut, skinned and grated +
$^{1}/_{3}$ tsp salt, steamed for 10 minutes and
set aside

- Place glutinous rice flour in a mixing bowl and gradually add *pandan* leaf water while kneading mixture. Add slaked lime water and continue to knead until dough is malleable and no longer sticky.

- Bring a pot of water to the boil.

- Pinch out enough dough to make a marble-size ball. Flatten and fill with $^{1}/_{4}$ tsp palm sugar, then gather up edges of dough to enclose sugar and reshape into a ball. Immediately lower glutinous rice ball into rapidly boiling water and cook until it floats to the surface. Remove with a slotted spoon and leave to drain.

- Repeat step until all ingredients are used up.

- Roll balls in steamed grated coconut and serve.

NOTE:

If fresh pandan and suji leaves are not available, add 1–2 drops green pandan extract or green food colouring to 5 Tbsp water and stir to mix well.

glutinous**rice**flourcakes

300 ml (10 fl oz / 1¼ cups) coconut milk, extracted from 1 grated coconut

125 g (4½ oz) black glutinous rice flour

250 g (9 oz) white glutinous rice flour

½ tsp salt

30 banana leaves, trimmed to make 15-cm (6-in) diameter rounds and greased with cooking oil

Bamboo skewers to secure

Coconut Filling

350 g (12½ oz) skinned and grated young coconut

200 g (7 oz) sugar

1 tsp vanilla extract or ¼ tsp ground vanilla

150 ml (5 fl oz / ⅔ cup) water

Salt to taste

Coconut Sauce

350 ml (11⅔ fl oz / 1⅖ cups) coconut milk, extracted from 1 grated coconut + a pinch of salt

- Heat coconut milk and bring to the boil.

- In a mixing bowl, combine both types of glutinous rice flours and salt. Pour in boiling coconut milk and stir with wooden spoon until well mixed. When cool enough to handle, knead mixture until it is malleable. Divide into 30 equal portions. Set aside.

- Prepare coconut filling. In a medium pot, combine all ingredients and simmer over low heat, stirring constantly, until all liquid is absorbed. Divide into 30 equal portions.

- To assemble a banana leaf parcel, take a portion of rice flour dough and roll into a ball, then flatten into a round and place a portion of coconut filling in the centre. Gather up edges of dough to enclose and seal, then roll back into a ball.

- Fold a piece of banana leaf, greased side facing inwards, into a cone and insert dough ball. Spoon 2–3 Tbsp coconut sauce into cone, then fold in rim of banana leaf cone to enclose filling and form a pyramid-shaped parcel. Secure with a skewer. Repeat until all ingredients are used up.

- Steam parcels for about 45 minutes until cooked.

53

rice flour balls in coconut sauce

250 g (9 oz) glutinous rice flour

50 g (1²/₃ oz) sago flour

225 ml (7¹/₂ fl oz / 1 cup) water + ¹/₂ tsp salt, stirred until salt has dissolved

1–2 drops each red and green food colouring

2 *pandan* leaves, cut into 3-cm (1¹/₂-in) patterned strips

50 banana leaves for making parcels (*tum*), each 20 x 30-cm (8 x12-in)

Bamboo skewers

Coconut Sauce

450 ml (15 fl oz / 1⁴/₅ cups) coconut milk, extracted from 1 grated coconut

1¹/₂ tsp rice flour

1 tsp salt

Filling

¹/₂ young coconut, skinned and grated

150 g (5¹/₃ oz) palm sugar, finely grated

100 ml (3¹/₂ fl oz/ ²/₅ cup) water

¹/₂ tsp salt

1 *pandan* leaf, knotted

- Prepare coconut sauce. Combine all ingredients and set aside.

- Prepare filling. In a medium pot, combine all ingredients and simmer over low heat until liquid is absorbed. When cool enough to handle, divide into 50 portions and shape into balls.

- In a mixing bowl, combine glutinous rice and sago flours. Gradually add water and knead constantly until mixture is malleable. Halve dough into 2 equal parts; colour 1 portion with red food colouring and the other, green. Roll pink-coloured dough into a long rope and cut into 25 equal parts, then roll into balls. Repeat step with green coloured dough.

- Flatten a dough ball into a disc and place a portion of filling in the centre. Gather up edges of dough to enclose and seal, then roll into a ball again. Repeat until all 50 balls of dough are filled.

- Assemble parcels. Stack 2 banana leaves together, with shiny sides facing outwards. Place 1 green glutinous rice ball, 1 pink glutinous rice ball and a strip of pandan leaf in the centre.

- Wrap and fold leaves into a *tum* parcel (page 11). Stir coconut sauce again before using. Spoon 3–4 Tbsp coconut sauce into parcel and secure with a bamboo skewer. Repeat until all ingredients are used up.

- Steam for about 15 minutes until cooked. Serve as desired.

mochi

500 g (1 lb 1½ oz) glutinous rice flour

750 ml (24 fl oz / 3 cups) water

100 ml (3½ fl oz / ⅖ cup) coconut milk, extracted from ½ grated coconut

½ tsp salt

2 drops rose essence

1–2 drops food colouring of choice

Flour for Coating

50 g (1⅔ oz) corn flour (cornstarch)

1 *pandan* leaf, cut into 3-cm (1½-in) strips

Filling

100 g (3½ oz) blanched peanuts, dry-roasted

50 g (1⅔ oz) sugar

2 Tbsp white sesame seeds, toasted

- Prepare filling. Grind all ingredients together until fine. Set aside.

- Prepare flour for coating. In a nonstick frying pan, stir-fry corn flour and *pandan* leaf without oil for about 10 minutes until fragrant. Discard *pandan* leaf and set aside.

- Place glutinous rice flour in a large mixing bowl lined with a large sheet of muslin cloth. Gradually add water and combine mixture. Gather up edges of muslin cloth and squeeze to strain liquid from flour mixture. Transfer drained flour mixture to new mixing bowl. Gradually add coconut milk and knead until dough is malleable and no longer sticky.

- Divide dough into 4 equal parts if making rice flour cakes in 4 different colours. Colour each part of dough as desired and knead again to colour dough evenly.

- Steam coloured mixtures in 4 separate heatproof (flameproof) greased tins for 30 minutes until cooked. Remove and leave to cool slightly.

- Pinch out enough dough to form a ball the size of a ping pong ball. Place dough ball on a small sheet of cling film and make a well at the centre of dough. Spoon 1 Tbsp filling into well and gather up edges of cling wrap to roll dough back into a smooth ball. Remove cling film and coat ball with corn flour, shaking off any excess. Repeat until all ingredients are used up.

- Serve immediately or store glutinous rice flour cakes in airtight containers to prevent them from becoming dry and hard.

custardricecakes

Glutinous Rice Layer

Cooking oil for greasing tin

250 ml (8 fl oz / 1 cup) coconut milk, extracted from ½ grated coconut

1 *pandan* leaf, knotted

½ tsp salt

250 g (9 oz) white glutinous rice, soaked for 2 hours and drained

Custard Layer

6 eggs

175 g (6 oz) sugar

15 *suji* leaves blended with 3½ Tbsp water, liquid strained

300 ml (10 fl oz / 1¼ cups) coconut cream, extracted from 1 grated coconut

3 Tbsp rice flour

¼ tsp salt

- Grease a 22 x 6-cm (9 x 2½-in) square tin. Set aside.

- Prepare glutinous rice layer. In a large pot, combine coconut milk, *pandan* leaf and salt. Simmer over medium heat and add glutinous rice. Cook over low heat until coconut milk is fully absorbed by rice grains. Discard *pandan* leaf. Transfer rice to prepared tin. Compact rice in tin by pressing down with the back of a spoon. Steam in a preheated steamer for about 10 minutes.

- Prepare custard layer. Gently whisk eggs and sugar with a fork until combined. Add remaining ingredients and stir until combined. Pour mixture on top of glutinous rice layer.

- Return tin to steamer and steam over medium heat for about 45 minutes until custard layer is set and cooked. Remove and leave to cool. Cut and serve as desired.

NOTE:

If fresh suji leaves are not available, add 1–2 drops green food colouring to 50 ml (1²/₃ fl oz / ¼ cup) water and stir to mix well.

mungbeancakes

300 ml (10 fl oz / 1¹/₄ cups) coconut milk, extracted from 1 grated coconut

250 g (9 oz) glutinous rice flour

100 g (3¹/₂ oz) castor sugar

¹/₄ tsp salt

1–2 drops food colouring of choice

Banana leaves, cut into squares or circles the size of cake mould and brushed with cooking oil

Cooking oil for greasing moulds

Filling

200 g (7 oz) skinned mung beans, steamed until cooked and mashed

175 g (6 oz) sugar

100 ml (3¹/₂ fl oz / ²/₅ cup) coconut milk, extracted from ¹/₂ grated coconut

¹/₄ tsp salt

2 tsp vanilla extract or ¹/₂ tsp ground vanilla

- Prepare filling. In a large nonstick frying pan, combine all ingredients and simmer over low heat, stirring constantly, until liquid is absorbed and mixture is malleable.

- When cool enough to handle, take 2–3 Tbsp mixture and roll into a ball. Repeat until green bean paste is used up. Set aside.

- Simmer coconut milk over low heat until warm. In a mixing bowl, combine glutinous rice and sago flours, sugar and salt. Gradually add warmed coconut milk and knead constantly until mixture is malleable and no longer sticky.

- Divide into 2 equal portions and colour each portion as desired. Knead to ensure dough is evenly coloured.

- Divide both portions of dough into balls large enough to fit snugly into mould.

- To assemble, form a well in a ball of dough, then place a ball of filling inside and gather edges of dough to enclose and reseal. Grease mould with oil. Press filled dough into mould firmly to ensure that patterns are well imprinted onto cake. Gently knock mould against work surface to dislodge cake and place on a piece of greased banana leaf. Repeat until all ingredients are used up.

- Steam cakes over medium heat for about 15 minutes until cooked.

baked**rice**flour**cake**

450 ml (15 fl oz / $1^4/5$ cups) coconut milk,
extracted from $^1/_2$ grated coconut

250 g (9 oz) sugar

$^1/_4$ tsp salt

2 tsp vanilla extract or $^1/_2$ tsp ground
vanilla

250 g (9 oz) glutinous rice flour

$^1/_3$ young coconut, skinned and grated

- Preheat oven to 180°C (350°F).

- Line a 23 x 3-cm (9 x $1^1/_2$-in) square tin with greased banana leaves. Set aside.

- In a medium pot, combine coconut milk and sugar. Stirring constantly, heat and bring to the boil. Remove from heat when sugar has dissolved totally. Stir in salt and vanilla. Leave to cool.

- In a mixing bowl, combine glutinous rice flour and grated coconut. Gradually add coconut milk and stir constantly until mixture is combined. Transfer mixture to prepared tin.

- Place in preheated oven and bake for about 40 minutes until cooked and golden brown in colour. Remove and leave to cool. Cut as desired and serve.

friedriceflourballs

250 g (9 oz) glutinous rice flour

25 g ($^3/_4$ oz) sago flour

$^1/_4$ tsp salt

175 ml (6 fl oz / $^3/_4$ cup) warm coconut milk, extracted from $^1/_4$ grated coconut with sufficient warm water added

100 g (3$^1/_2$ oz) white sesame seeds, washed, drained and air-dried

Cooking oil for deep-frying

Filling

200 g (7 oz) skinned mung beans, soaked for 1 hour and drained

150 g (5$^1/_3$ oz) sugar

1 *pandan* leaf, knotted

50 ml (1$^2/_3$ fl oz / $^1/_4$ cup) coconut milk, extracted from $^1/_8$ grated coconut

- Prepare filling. Steam mung beans over medium heat for 1 hour until cooked. Remove and mash while still hot. In a medium pot, combine mashed mung beans with remaining ingredients. Simmer over low heat, stirring constantly until all liquid has been absorbed and mixture is malleable. Remove and leave to cool. Roll bean paste into 1.5-cm (1-in) diameter balls and set aside.

- In a mixing bowl, combine glutinous rice and sago flours and salt. Gradually add warm coconut milk and knead constantly until mixture is malleable. Divide into 12 equal portions.

- Roll a portion of dough into a ball and make a well in the centre. Place a ball of filling into well, then gather edges of dough to enclose and reseal. Reshape into a ball. Repeat until all ingredients are used up.

- Coat each glutinous rice flour ball with sesame seeds, pressing slightly to ensure that sesame seeds adhere.

- Heat oil for deep-frying. Deep-fry glutinous rice flour balls until cooked and golden brown in colour. Remove with a slotted spoon and drain on paper towels before serving.

layered rice cakes

1 kg (2 lb 3 oz) white glutinous rice, soaked for 2–3 hours and drained

5 *suji* leaves, pounded + 1 Tbsp water, liquid extracted

5-cm (2-in) knob turmeric, peeled, grated and juice extracted for use

Spice Paste

6 shallots, peeled

3 cloves garlic, peeled

1 tsp salt

1 tsp coriander seeds

1/4 tsp cumin seeds

2 candlenuts

Filling

3 Tbsp cooking oil

1 small chicken, cooked, skinned, boned and meat shredded for use

2 kaffir lime leaves

1 lemongrass, bruised

350 ml (11^2/$_3$ fl oz / 1^2/$_5$ cups) coconut milk, extracted from 1/2 grated coconut

2 Tbsp grated palm sugar

1/2 tsp tamarind paste

1 tsp rice flour or plain (all-purpose) flour

Coconut Milk Mixture

350 ml (11^2/$_3$ fl oz / 1^2/$_5$ cups) coconut milk, extracted from 1^1/$_2$ grated coconuts

1 tsp salt

2 *pandan* leaves, knotted

- Prepare spice paste. Grind all ingredients together until fine.

- Prepare filling. In a large frying pan, heat oil and fry spice paste for 2–3 minutes until fragrant. Except rice flour or plain flour, add all remaining ingredients and cook over medium heat, stirring occasionally, until all liquid has been absorbed. Before removing from heat, sprinkle on rice flour or plain flour and stir to combine well. Discard kaffir lime leaves and lemongrass. Divide into 2 equal portions. Set aside.

- Steam glutinous rice over medium heat for about 15 minutes and remove from steamer.

- Prepare coconut milk mixture. In a small pot, combine all ingredients and bring to the boil. Remove and divide into 3 equal parts.

- Divide steamed glutinous rice into 3 equal parts. In 3 separate mixing bowls, add a portion of hot coconut milk to each portion of glutinous rice and stir to combine.

- Add *suji* leaf liquid to 1 portion of glutinous rice mixture to colour it green. Add turmeric juice to the second portion of glutinous rice to colour it yellow. Leave the third portion plain. Stir all 3 portions separately until coconut milk has been fully absorbed.

- Steam all 3 portions of glutinous rice mixture for 20–30 minutes each until cooked.

- Assemble layered rice cake. Line a 10 x 25-cm (4 x 10-in) square tin with greased banana leaves. Spoon green coloured glutinous rice into tin and press down with the back of spoon to form a 1-cm (½-in) thick layer. Spoon and spread a layer of chicken filling evenly on top, then add on a layer of yellow coloured rice.

- Continue to alternate between the different coloured rice layers and chicken filling until all ingredients are used up. Leave to cool completely. Cut and serve as desired.

NOTE:

If fresh suji leaves are not available, add a tiny drop of green food colouring to 1 Tbsp water and stir to mix well.

greenbananas

200 g (7 oz) rice flour

400 ml (13^1/$_3$ fl oz / 1^3/$_4$ cup) coconut milk, extracted from 1 grated coconut

50 g (1^2/$_3$ oz) sugar

Salt to taste

50 ml (1^2/$_3$ fl oz / ^{1}/$_4$ cup) *suji* or *pandan* leaf extract

10 banana leaves, cut into size large enough to enlose bananas

50 ml (1^2/$_3$ fl oz / ^{1}/$_4$ cup) coconut cream, extracted from ^{1}/$_4$ grated coconut

10 ripe bananas (*raja* or *kepuk*), peeled and steamed

Coconut Milk Sauce

35 g (1 oz) rice flour

100 g (3^1/$_2$ oz) sugar

500 ml (16 fl oz / 2 cups) coconut milk extracted from ^{1}/$_2$ grated coconut

^{1}/$_2$ tsp salt

- Mix rice flour, coconut milk, sugar, salt and *suji* or *pandan* leaf extract. Place over low heat and stir evenly until mixture is thick. Leave to cool.

- Brush a banana leaf with coconut cream, then spoon 3 Tbsp dough on leaf. Press dough down into an even thickness (about 0.5-cm / ^{1}/$_4$-in), and place a banana on it. Wrap dough over banana to enclose it. Wrap with banana leaf and let parcel sit on open ends of leaf in steamer. Repeat until ingredients are used up.

- Steam for 10 minutes.

- Prepare coconut milk sauce. Mix all ingredients and bring to boil. Cook until sauce thickens slightly.

- Serve green bananas drizzled with coconut milk sauce.

sweet**sago**dessert

50 g (1²/₃ oz) mung bean flour

850 ml (27¹/₂ fl oz / 3²/₅ cups) coconut milk, extracted from 1 grated coconut

100 g (3¹/₂ oz) red-coloured sago pearls

1 *pandan* leaf, knotted

¹/₂ tsp salt

200 g (7 oz) sugar

15 banana leaves or clear plastic sheets for wrapping, each 15 x 15-cm (6 x 6-in)

- In a mixing bowl, combine mung bean flour with 450 ml (15 fl oz / 1⁴/₅ cups) coconut milk and stir until flour dissolves completely. Set aside.

- In a medium pot, combine sago pearls, 400 ml (13¹/₃ fl oz / 1³/₄ cups) coconut milk, salt and *pandan* leaf. Simmer over medium heat, stirring constantly until sago pearls turn translucent and are cooked. Add sugar, then reduce heat and cook, stirring constantly until sugar has dissolved totally. Discard *pandan* leaf and continue to simmer over low heat.

- Stir mung bean flour mixture again and immediately pour into simmering sago pearl mixture. Cook, stirring constantly until mixture thickens.

- To assemble, spoon 1–2 Tbsp mixture onto centre of a banana leaf or plastic sheet. Wrap up to form a neat parcel and tuck the ends underneath so the weight of parcel rests on them. Repeat until all ingredients are used up. Leave to set completely. Serve at room temperature or chilled.

marbledcakes

125 g (4½ oz) mung bean flour

1 litre (32 fl oz / 4 cups) coconut milk, extracted from 1½ grated coconuts

175 g (6 oz) sugar

2 tsp vanilla extract or ½ tsp ground vanilla

½ tsp salt

1½ Tbsp chocolate powder + 50 ml (1⅔ fl oz / ¼ cup) hot water, mixed and stir until dissolved

- In a mixing bowl, combine mung bean flour with 500ml (16 fl oz / 2 cups) coconut milk. Stir until flour has dissolved.

- In a medium pot, heat remaining coconut milk with sugar, vanilla and salt over low heat and bring to a simmer. Stir in mung bean flour-coconut milk mixture and cook until mixture thickens.

- In a small pot, add a ladleful of white-coloured mung bean flour mixture. Stir in liquid chocolate and bring to the boil. Remove from heat.

- Sprinkle a 20 x 20 x 5-cm (8 x 8 x 2-in) tin with water. Transfer white-coloured mixture to prepared tin and level surface with the back of a spoon. Ladle chocolate mixture on top. Stir with a bamboo skewer or fork while rotating skewer or fork at the same time to produce a marble effect. Leave to set completely. Cut and serve as desired.

sagoflourcakes

275 g (9 4/5 oz) sago flour

2 Tbsp cold water

100 ml (3 1/2 fl oz / 2/5 cup) boiling water

1–2 drops food colouring of choice

1/4 young coconut, skinned and grated +
1/4 tsp salt, steamed for 10 minutes

100 g (3 1/2 oz) sugar

- Dissolve 1 Tbsp sago flour in 2 Tbsp cold water.

- In a mixing bowl, combine sago flour mixture and boiling water. Stir until mixture thickens. Add remaining sago flour and stir by hand until mixture becomes malleable. Divide mixture into 3 or 4 parts and colour each portion of dough as desired.

- Bring a large pot of water to the boil. Roll a portion of coloured dough into a long thin rope and cut into equal lengths. Repeat with remaining portions of dough.

- Cook lengths of dough in boiling water until they float to the surface. Remove with a slotted spoon and drain briefly before coating with grated coconut.

- Arrange cakes on small serving plates or banana leaf cups. Sprinkle sugar on top and serve.

rolledpancakes

150 g (5¹/₃ oz) plain (all-purpose) flour, sifted

1 egg

¹/₄ tsp salt

200 ml (7 fl oz / ³/₄ cup) coconut milk, extracted from ¹/₂ grated coconut

3 *pandan* leaves + 5 *suji* leaves blended with 2 Tbsp water, liquid strained

1 Tbsp chocolate powder + 2 tsp hot water, stir until dissolved

1–2 drops food colouring of choice

Coconut Filling

¹/₃ coconut, skinned and grated

150 g (5¹/₃ oz) palm sugar or 100 g (3¹/₂ oz) sugar

100 ml (3¹/₂ fl oz / ²/₅ cup) water

1 *pandan* leaf, knotted

¹/₄ tsp salt

- Prepare coconut filling. In a medium pot, combine all ingredients and cook over low heat. Stirring constantly, bring to the boil and simmer until all liquid has been absorbed. Remove and set aside to cool to room temperature.

- Prepare pancakes. In a mixing bowl, combine flour, egg and salt. Gradually add coconut milk, whisking constantly with a balloon whisk until mixture is smooth. If using an electric mixer, whisk at low speed until combined. Divide batter into 2 or 3 parts. Colour 1 portion with *suji-pandan* liquid, another portion with chocolate mixture and the third portion with food colouring of choice.

- Heat a 20-cm (10-in) diameter nonstick frying pan over low heat. Add 4 Tbsp batter to form a very thin pancake. Flip over when batter has set and cook briefly until done. Remove and place on a flat plate. Repeat until batter is used up. Set aside and leave to cool.

- Assemble pancakes. Place 1¹/₂–2 Tbsp coconut filling along centre of a pancake. Fold in sides to cover filling and roll up. Repeat until ingredients are used up.

NOTE:

If fresh suji and pandan leaves are not available, add 1 drop green food colouring or pandan extract to 2 Tbsp water and stir to mix well.

pancakes with
coconut sauce

150 g (5^1/$_3$ oz) plain (all-purpose) flour, sifted

1 tsp baking powder

1 egg

^{1}/$_4$ tsp salt

300 ml (10 fl oz / 1^1/$_4$ cups) coconut milk, extracted from 1 grated coconut

Coconut Sauce

250 ml (8 fl oz / 1 cup) coconut milk, extracted from ^{1}/$_4$ grated coconut

50 g (1^2/$_3$ oz) palm sugar, grated

1 tsp sugar

1 *pandan* leaf, knotted

1 tsp salt

- In a mixing bowl, add plain flour and make a well in the centre. Add baking powder, egg and salt into well. Using an electric mixer, whisk at low speed to combine ingredients briefly. Increase mixer speed to medium and gradually add coconut milk. Whisk until mixture is combined and smooth.

- Heat a small nonstick frying pan over medium heat until slightly smoking. Add about 3 Tbsp batter to form a pancake. When tiny holes appear on surface of pancake, lower heat and cover frying pan briefly for 1–2 minutes until pancake is cooked. Remove to a plate and repeat until batter is used up.

- Prepare coconut sauce. In a small pot, combine all ingredients. Cook over low heat, stirring constantly and bring to the boil. Remove from heat and discard *pandan* leaf. Set aside to cool.

- Serve pancakes with coconut sauce.

NOTE:

Make the coconut sauce more flavourful by adding about 50 g (1^2/$_3$ oz) finely diced jackfruit flesh or blended durian flesh.

sweetcrepes

1 tsp instant yeast

375 ml (12 fl oz / 1½ cups) coconut milk
extracted from ½ coconut, warmed

250 g (9 oz) plain (all-purpose) flour

150 g (5⅓ oz) sugar

2 eggs

¼ tsp baking soda

Margarine for brushing pan

Topping (to taste)

Skinned peanuts, toasted and chopped

White sesame seeds, toasted

Sugar

Chocolate rice

Sweetened condensed milk

Fruit jam

- Add yeast to warm coconut milk and stir until yeast is dissolved and mixture is foamy. Set aside.

- Mix flour and sugar, then make a hole in the centre. Add eggs. Stir while adding yeast-and-coconut milk mixture until batter is well-mixed and sugar is dissolved. Add baking soda and stir again until smooth. Set aside in a warm place for about 15 minutes.

- Heat a small nonstick frying pan over medium heat until slightly smoking. Brush with margarine. Add about 3 Tbsp batter to form a pancake and cook until it rises. Before the surface dries, add topping ingredients as desired and fold pancake in half.

- Repeat with remaining ingredients. Serve warm.

Indonesianwaffles

400 g (14 oz) plain (all-purpose) flour

1 level Tbsp instant yeast

2 tsp vanilla extract or $^1/_2$ tsp ground vanilla

$^1/_2$ tsp salt

400 ml ($13^1/_3$ fl oz / $1^3/_4$ cups) coconut milk, extracted from $1^1/_2$ grated coconuts

6 eggs + 275 g ($9^4/_5$ oz) sugar, whisked until sugar has dissolved

Margarine for greasing mould

- In a mixing bowl, combine flour, yeast, vanilla and salt. Gradually add chilled coconut milk while whisking mixture with an electric mixer at low speed. Whisk for about 5 minutes until mixture is smooth.

- Add eggs and sugar mixture to flour mixture and whisk until thoroughly combined. Cover bowl with a damp tea towel and set aside for about 1 hour until mixture doubles in volume.

- Heat a waffle mould and grease with margarine. Pour batter into mould until full, then close and cook waffles until golden brown in colour. Remove cooked waffle and repeat until batter is used up. Serve warm.

Indonesianmuffins

$^1/_2$ tsp instant yeast

4 Tbsp warm water

2 tsp sugar

2 eggs

1 egg white

150 g (5$^1/_3$ oz) plain (all-purpose) flour, sifted

150 ml (5 fl oz / $^3/_5$ cup) coconut cream

Margarine for greasing moulds

Filling (to taste)

Grated cheese, banana slices, chocolate rice or corned beef

- Mix yeast with warm water and set aside.

- Using an electric mixer, whisk sugar, eggs and egg white in a mixing bowl until doubled in volume. Fold in flour in small batches until combined.

- Fold in yeast mixture, then gradually add coconut cream and whisk until combined. Cover bowl and leave in a dry and warm place until batter is almost doubled in volume.

- Heat moulds and grease liberally with margarine. Fill each mould with batter until two-thirds full, then top batter with some grated cheese, banana slices, chocolate rice or corned beef as desired. Cook until cakes rise and are done.

- Repeat until ingredients are used up.

mudcakes

250 ml (8 fl oz / 1 cup) water

75 g (2²/₃ oz) margarine

150 g (5¹/₃ oz) plain (all-purpose) flour

125 g (4¹/₂ oz) sugar

¹/₄ tsp salt

2 tsp vanilla extract or ¹/₂ tsp ground vanilla

5 eggs

450 ml (15 fl oz / 1⁴/₅ cups) coconut milk, extracted from 1 grated coconut, boiled and left to cool before chilling in fridge

Cooking oil for greasing moulds

100 g (3¹/₂ oz) raisins

¹/₂ young coconut, flesh removed and sliced into strips

- In a medium pot, bring water to the boil over low heat. Stir in margarine to dissolve, then add the whole portion of flour and stir evenly with a wooden spoon. Add sugar, salt and vanilla. Stir evenly, then remove from heat and leave to cool.

- When batter is cool, stir in eggs one by one until combined. Gradually add coconut milk, stirring constantly, until mixture is smooth and combined.

- Heat mud cake moulds on a stove hob and grease with oil.

- Fill moulds with batter until one-third full. Cover and cook for 5–7 minutes until cakes are half-done, then uncover and sprinkle some raisins and place a few strips of young coconut flesh on top of each cake. Cover again and cook for another 5 minutes until cakes are done. Remove from moulds and serve.

mini**sponge**cakes

3 eggs

150 g (5$^1/_3$ oz) sugar

$^1/_2$ tsp *pandan* essence

150 g (5$^1/_3$ oz) plain (all-purpose) flour +
$^1/_2$ tsp baking powder, sifted

100 ml (3$^1/_2$ fl oz / $^2/_5$ cup) coconut cream

5 *suji* leaves blended with 2 Tbsp water, liquid
strained

$^1/_8$ tsp salt

Cooking oil for greasing moulds

- Preheat a steamer with sufficient boiling water over high heat.

- Using an electric mixer, whisk eggs, sugar and *pandan* essence until thick and doubled in volume.

- Gradually fold in flour in small batches with a rubber spatula until combined. Gradually and gently fold in coconut cream until mixture is smooth. Finally, fold in *suji* leaf liquid and salt until batter is evenly coloured.

- Grease cake moulds of 50 ml (1$^2/_3$ fl oz / $^1/_4$ cup) capacity with oil and fill with batter until two-thirds full. Steam in preheated steamer for 20 minutes until cakes are done.

NOTE:

If fresh suji leaves are not available, add 1 drop green food colouring to 2 Tbsp water and stir to mix well.

chickenpancakes

10 *salam* leaves or bay leaves to place in each parcel of banana leaves for wrapping

20 banana leaves for wrapping, each 20 x 30-cm (8 x 12-in)

Spice Paste

5 shallots, peeled

2 cloves garlic, peeled

2 tsp coriander seeds, toasted

1/4 tsp cumin seeds, toasted

1 tsp white peppercorns

Coconut Sauce

500 ml (16 fl oz / 2 cups) coconut milk, extracted from 1 grated coconut

1 Tbsp rice or plain (all-purpose) flour

1/2 tsp salt

Filling

2 Tbsp cooking oil for stir-frying

300 g (11 oz) minced chicken

1/2 tsp salt or to taste

2 tsp sugar or to taste

100 ml (3 1/2 fl oz / 2/5 cup) coconut cream

1/2 chayote, peeled and roughly grated

Pancakes

250 g (9 oz) plain (all-purpose) flour

1/4 tsp salt

2 eggs, briefly whisked

500 ml (16 fl oz / 2 cups) coconut milk, extracted from 1/4 grated coconut

2 Tbsp cooking oil

- Prepare spice paste. Grind all ingredients together to a fine mixture. Set aside.

- Prepare coconut sauce. In a mixing bowl, combine all ingredients and stir until mixture is smooth.

- Prepare pancakes. In a mixing bowl, combine flour, salt and eggs. Gradually add coconut milk while whisking with an electric mixer at low speed. Whisk until mixture is smooth. Add cooking oil to batter and stir to mix well.

- Heat an 18-cm (7-in) diameter frying pan. Add 3–4 Tbsp batter to pan to make a thin pancake. Flip over when set to cook other side. Remove to a plate. Repeat until batter is used up.

- Prepare filling. Heat oil and fry spice paste until fragrant. Add minced chicken, salt and sugar and stir-fry briefly. Stir in coconut cream and add chayote. Cook over low heat, stirring occasionally until most of the liquid has been absorbed.

- Assemble wrapped pancakes. Place 1¹/₂–2 Tbsp chicken filling along centre of a pancake. Fold in sides to enclose filling and form a rectangular parcel. Repeat until ingredients are used up.

- Stack 2 banana leaves together, with shiny sides facing outwards. Place a *salam* leaf on top, followed by a wrapped pancake. Wrap and fold leaves into a *tum* parcel (page 11). Spoon 2 Tbsp coconut sauce into parcel and secure with a bamboo skewer. Repeat until all ingredients are used up. Steam for about

tunabread

Bread Dough

250 g (9 oz) plain (all-purpose) flour

1 egg, lightly whisked

1½ Tbsp sugar

¼ tsp salt

1 tsp instant yeast + 1½ Tbsp warm water,
stir until dissolved

Spice Paste

5 shallots, peeled

1 clove garlic, peeled

5 large red chillies

2 candlenuts, toasted

1 tsp minced ginger

Salt and sugar, to taste

Filling

Cooking oil as needed

200 g (7 oz) fresh tuna fillet

1 Tbsp lime juice or tamarind juice

3 Tbsp cooking oil for stir-frying

1 tomato, finely chopped

250 ml (8 fl oz / 1 cup) coconut milk,
extracted from 1 grated coconut

3 kaffir lime leaves, finely shredded

25 g (¾ oz) basil leaves, shredded

- Prepare spice paste. Grind all ingredients together until fine. Set aside.

- Marinate tuna with lime or tamarind juice and steam or bake until cooked. Remove and mince roughly.

- Prepare filling. Heat oil and stir-fry spice paste until fragrant. Add tomato, minced fish, coconut milk and kaffir lime leaves. Simmer, stirring occasionally, until all liquid has been absorbed. Stir in basil leaves and remove from heat. Set aside to cool.

- Prepare bread dough. In a mixing bowl, add flour and make a well in the centre. Add egg, sugar and salt into well and slowly combine with hand. Gradually add yeast mixture, kneading constantly for about 30 minutes until dough no longer sticks to your hands. Roll dough into a ball and leave in mixing bowl. Cover with a tea towel and set aside in a warm place for 1–2 hours until dough has doubled in volume.

- Assemble tuna-filled bread. Roll dough into a long rope and divide into 12–14 equal parts. Roll a portion of dough into a ball and flatten into a 0.5-cm (¼-in) thick disc. Spoon 1–2 tsp tuna filling in the centre. Fold dough over to enclose filling and twist edges to seal. Place on a greased baking tray. Repeat until ingredients are used up. Leave completed buns to proof for another 10 minutes before deep-frying.

- Heat oil for deep-frying. Deep-fry bread until golden brown in colour. Drain on paper towels and serve.

steamedcassavacakes

1 kg (2 lb 3 oz) cassava (tapioca), peeled and grated

200 g (7 oz) sugar

1 tsp salt

2 tsp vanilla extract or $1/2$ tsp ground vanilla

1–2 drops food colouring of choice

1 young coconut, skinned and grated + $1/2$ tsp salt, steamed for 10 minutes

- In a mixing bowl, combine cassava, sugar, salt and vanilla. Divide mixture into 3 or 4 parts, and colour each part with 1–2 drops food colouring as desired.

- Line steaming disc with banana leaves. Press and stack layers of different coloured cassava mixture together on banana leaves to obtain a multi-coloured cake. Alternatively, steam each coloured portion of cassava mixture in small tins separately.

- Steam for about 45 minutes until cake or cakes are cooked. Remove and leave to cool. Cut into desired shapes, then coat with grated coconut and serve.

NOTE:

Steaming grated coconut with a pinch of salt helps to prevent the coconut from spoiling easily.

cassavaincoconutmilk

1 kg (2 lb 3 oz) cassava (tapioca),
peeled and cut to 5-cm (2-in) lengths,
then halved lengthways

350 ml (11^2/$_3$ fl oz / 1^2/$_5$ cups) water

^{1}/$_2$ tsp salt

5 *pandan* leaves, knotted

100 g (3^1/$_2$ oz) sugar

250 ml (8 fl oz / 1 cup) coconut milk,
extracted from 1 grated coconut

1 tsp corn flour (cornstarch), dissolved
in a little water

- In a medium pot, add cassava, water, salt and *pandan* leaves. Cook over medium heat and bring to the boil, then lower heat and simmer until cassava is cooked.

- In a mixing bowl, combine sugar, coconut milk and corn flour mixture, until sugar has dissolved.

- Gradually add combined coconut milk to cooked cassava mixture, stirring constantly until sauce has thickened. Remove from heat and serve when cool.

sweetpotatocakes

Sweet Potato Layer

300 g (11 oz) sweet potatoes, steamed, peeled and mashed

60 g (2$^1/_6$ oz) corn flour (cornstarch)

150 ml (5 fl oz / $^3/_5$ cup) coconut milk, extracted from $^1/_2$ grated coconut

100 g (3$^1/_2$ oz) sugar

$^1/_4$ tsp salt

Cooking oil for greasing bowls

Coconut Milk Layer

400 ml (13$^1/_3$ fl oz / 1$^3/_4$ cups) coconut milk

50 g (1$^2/_3$ oz) sugar

5 Tbsp water

50 g (1$^2/_3$ oz) corn flour (cornstarch)

$^1/_4$ tsp salt

- Preheat steamer with sufficient boiling water over medium heat.

- Prepare coconut milk layer. In a medium pot, combine all ingredients until well mixed. Cook over medium heat, stirring constantly, until mixture is thick and smooth. Remove and set aside.

- Prepare sweet potato layer. In a mixing bowl, combine all ingredients until well mixed. Put mixture through a metal sieve to obtain a really smooth paste.

- Grease small heatproof (flameproof) bowls with oil. Fill bowls until two-thirds full with sweet potato mixture and level surfaces with back of spoon. Place in steamer and steam for 10 minutes. When sweet potato mixtures have set slightly, pour coconut milk mixture on top to fill bowls. Steam again for about 10 minutes until cooked through. Decorate as desired and serve.

corncakes

6 ears young corn, silk removed and
discarded, husks removed and set aside
for wrapping

$^1/_3$ young coconut, skinned and grated

100 g (3$^1/_2$ oz) sugar

1 tsp vanilla extract or $^1/_4$ tsp ground vanilla

$^1/_2$ tsp salt

- Rinse corn cobs, then drain and set aside. Separate husks into individual leaves, rinse and set aside.

- Grate corn off cobs finely. In a mixing bowl, add grated corn with all remaining ingredients and stir to combine well.

- Spoon 1–2 Tbsp corn mixture into a leaf of corn husk and roll into a long tube to enclose filling. Repeat until mixture is used up. Steam corn cakes for 30 minutes until cooked. Remove and leave to cool. Serve.

NOTE:

After steaming, the corn husk wrappings may become wrinkled and turn yellow in colour. If you wish to present these cakes in more attractive wrappers, replace the used leaves with new leaves that have been briefly blanched in boiling water.

cassava patties

500 g (1 lb 1¹/₂ oz) cassava (tapioca),
peeled and grated

1 tsp salt

Cooking oil for deep-frying

Filling

1 Tbsp cooking oil for frying

200 g (7 oz) fermented soy bean cake
(*tempe*), rinsed and mashed with a fork

100 ml (3¹/₂ fl oz / ²/₅ cup) water

1 spring onion (scallion), finely sliced

Spice Paste

4 small red chillies

2 large red chillies

2 cloves of garlic, peeled

4 shallots, peeled

1 tsp salt or to taste

1 Tbsp sugar or to taste

- Prepare spice paste. Grind all ingredients together until fine. Set aside.

- Prepare filing. In a large frying pan, heat oil and stir-fry spice paste until fragrant.

- Add mashed fermented soy bean cake and stir-fry for 1–2 minutes, then add water and simmer until liquid has been absorbed. Finally, stir in spring onion and remove from heat. Set aside to cool.

- In a mixing bowl, combine grated cassava and salt. Take 1–2 Tbsp mixture, then shape and roll into a ball. Make a well in the centre. Spoon 1–2 Tbsp filling inside and seal. Shape into a patty. Repeat until ingredients are used up.

- Heat oil for deep-frying. Deep-fry patties in batches until cooked and golden brown. Drain on paper towels and serve warm with small green chillies, if desired.

Yasa Boga, meaning "food maker" in Indonesian, is made up of a group of three homemakers who are also career women.

Hayatinufus A.L. Tobing, a former Coordinator of Culinary tests at a popular women's magazine, has spent twenty-five years in the culinary field. Her experiences range from teaching home economics in high schools and examining and creating new recipes to practising this art. Her experience and knowledge have contributed much to the high quality of this book.

Cherry Hadibroto, the founder of the Yasa Boga group, is responsible for the production quality of many cookbooks. An entrepreneur with many years of experience working for a women's magazine, she understands what people want from recipes and cookbooks, and meets those demands in this cookbook.

Nies Kartohadiprojo has the talent and experience of transforming all kinds of recipes into delicious dishes that look equally appetising. Since her retirement from a popular women's magazine, she now accepts special catering orders for parties and celebrations where her culinary powers are evident.